Also by Dave Hopwood:

Novels

The Twelfth Seer
- A big screen, action adventur

The Shed
- A disgruntled guy takes time out in a moorland monastery, crossing paths with rock stars, wanderers, world-changers and of course... monks

Dead Prophets Society
- A town turned upside-down by a gang of revolutionary punks

Sons of Thunder
- A contemporary gospel, the Messiah in Cornwall with surfers and mechanics for disciples

No More Heroes
- Cain, Solomon & Jacob in a modern tale of men, women, dads and crime

Other

Top Stories
- 31 parables retold with serious and humorous contemporary comments

Pulp Gospel
- 31 bits of the Bible retold with gritty reflections and comments

Rebel Yell: 31 Psalms
- Psalms, God & Rock'n'Roll

Faith & Film
- Movie clips that bring the Bible to life

The Bloke's Bible
- Bits of the Bible retold for guys

The Bloke's Bible 2: The Road Trip
- More Bible bits retold

31 Weird Places to Read a Bible
- Strange events in the Bible linked to our everyday lives

//Men 1 Boys//

Massive thanks to all those who have contributed to this project. And to Leigh Winsbury for inspiring this book. By the people for the people.

For more information visit Dave's website
davehopwood.com

Copyright © 2012 Dave Hopwood
All rights reserved.

//Men 2 Boys//

Men
& Boys

Thoughts about life from
A Few Good Men

Edited by
Dave Hopwood

//Men 3 Boys//

There is a time for everything.
A time to work and a time to play.
A time to talk and a time to listen.
A time to laugh and - yes - a time to cry.
A time to be cool and a time to be honest.

A time to be happy and a time to complain.
A time to rush and a time to wait.
A time for TV and a time for reality.
A time for loud music and a time for quiet.

A time to mess about and a time to knuckle down.
A time to respect, never a time to disrespect.
A time to chill and a time to get up at 6.00am.
A time to encourage and a time to be encouraged.

Based loosely on Ecclesiastes 3

//Men 4 Boys//

Hair

This is what happens when the irresistible force of nature meets the immovable object of puberty. Hair – it can't be stopped, it's like the terminator. Whatever you do to escape it, it will catch up on you. If you try to stop it, it comes back fighting harder the next time. Give in to it, celebrate it. Above all learn from this example – don't shave all your leg hair off in the bath, because the result is – stronger terminator hair in its place.

Hugh Webber

'I'll be back.'
Arnold Schwarzenegger, *The Terminator*

Top hairy men in history
The Hairy Bikers, the Yetty, Robert Plant in Led Zeppelin. Samson who never cut his hair till he was conned by Delilah into getting a number one cut. And Esau.
'My brother is a hairy man but I am smooth,' said Jacob, Esau's brother. Jacob was certainly smooth, he conned everybody. He even tried it on with an angel once.
(Genesis 32 v 22-32)

Dress down Friday

I think it has possibly taken me 30 years to become cool. What is meant to be a negative critique of my dress down Friday attire I take as a compliment, as an arrival at station cool, hip, sick, or whatever todays term is. Yes, today at the age of 42 I was compared to an 'ethnic rap dancer'. Result!

Hugh Webber

> John the Baptist's clothes were woven from camel hair, and he wore a leather belt; his food was locusts and wild honey. People came from miles around to the wilderness to hear him preach. His dressing down didn't get in the way of what mattered.
> Matthew 3 vv 4&5
> (John was part of that small group of guys, like Attila the Hun and Rupert the Bear, who had 'the' as a middle name)

Spots

The morning arrives and there it is – a volcano has somehow been transplanted on your face, or worse, two have arrived in perfect formation to really highlight your feelings of insecurity. What are the options? Return under the duvet, and fain illness, stick some spot cream on and pray for a miracle, or maybe, just maybe, if you squeezed its insides out it just wouldn't be there anymore – its worth a go isn't it?

Okay brace yourself as your fingers squeeze the little monster – come on rupture, burst. It seems to be getting redder and bigger, okay press on. Try another angle, surprise it from a different side, it's not working, it's never going to go. **BLAM!** The explosion hits the glass of the mirror, and seeing the guts of the creature lying dead there brings a very satisfying moment. You inspect the remains of the crater. Yes, I'm sure it's smaller, isn't it?

Hugh Webber – missiontowhereyouare.net

// Men 7 Boys //

> Those who suffer from any contagious skin disease must tear their clothes and loose their hair. Then, they must cover their mouth and wander about, calling out, 'Unclean! Unclean!'
> Leviticus 13 v 45

Or try *Clearasil* skin cream.

Dear Son,

I cried at your birth, you bawled at your baptism. You left a gigantic jobby on the stairs and applauded God for recycling food into poo! You scared me declaring 'Rangers' better than 'Morton'[1]! We converted to Killie FC[2] and sang *Paper Roses* on winning the Scottish Cup. You made friends easily and socialised at secondary school.

I can't remember being 15 going on 16, but I remember an elbow through glass, slamming doors, a bucket of water alarm clock, & puke out the window. At four you told a stranger he could die of smoking and 12 years later you lit up yourself. Debts grew, the truth came out and we moved on together. Despite the banter you're soft-hearted and quick to say, 'Sorry'. Now 22, you're respectful, stick at the low paid jobs and are rarely in! Your quick humour entertains and I enjoy your company.

// Men 9 Boys //

The road trip from Noddy's car to named driver has raced in. We've learned to forgive each other along the way and I want you to know for sure that I will always love you. I look forward to pursuing God's Adventure together & I am proud to call you my son.

Forever your Dad!

P.S. Snooker on Thursday?

[1] Greenock Morton FC
[2] Kilmarnock FC

> 'This is my beloved son, and I am totally pleased with him.'
> Matthew 3 v 17

Anonymous

> **From my son Josh in my birthday card:**
> 'Things Dad enjoys doing - football, swimming, emailing.'

How easy it is to be continually doing things, even family things, but not really doing anything together, and not really connecting. If there is one thing that my boys love and remember more than anything else it is doing things together, doing anything together, especially one to one. When you have more than one child, making time to do something with just one means a lot. My boys seem to be very different on their own with me than they are together.

Rev Will Kemp

Don't get me wrong, we have loads of fun all together, but often it's games, tasks, projects, competing with each other. When it is just the two of you, one to one, I see each one soften and become more open. Sitting and chatting is not always easy, especially if I am initiating and trying too hard to have a 'deep' conversation because I know this is the only time I have available this week (or this month!).

So it is generally best to be doing something, walking, going to the cinema, penalties, reading a book, even driving somewhere, but doing something and then the chatting, connecting, good questions etc just tend to happen; or not, it is OK either way, as long as we've had a bit of time just being together.

Rev Will Kemp

Top tip: Special Time

Just taking an hour after school one day a week for one parent to do something with one of the children. But they get to decide what we do. Activities vary a lot: football in the park; cafe - hot chocolate and a game (Uno, Guess Who, Chess); reading a book; treasure hunt in the garden; bike ride; playing on the Wii, etc

Rev Will Kemp

> Those who are wise will find a time and a way to do what is right. Yes, there is a time and a way for everything, though it's not always easy.
> Proverbs 8 vv 5&6

Between my garden and next door's there's a 6ft fence.
It marks the boundary between my property and his. No matter how much I want to wander in his garden and pick his flowers and vegetables, I can't because the fence stops me.

Boundaries are essential! I'm not just talking about 6ft fences, but boundaries in our lives – lines across which we will not step. They're particularly essential if we have a particular area of temptation where we're weak and give in easily – perhaps looking at harmful stuff on the internet, cheating on your girlfriend or wife, drinking one (or more) too many pints, and so on (you will know what your weakness is).

Andrew Robertson

My advice is to build a fence between you and that sin – a boundary over which you will not step. In the case of the internet this might be an electronic boundary, try www.covenanteyes.com but more importantly set a boundary (a guard) on your heart. (Proverbs 4:23). God Himself will patrol that boundary for you. The apostle John puts it like this, 'The One who is in you is greater than the one who is in the world.' (1 John 4:4).

Above all else, guard your heart, look after it, store good things in there. Patrol its doors and windows. Avoid stuffing it with corrosive substances, for it affects everything you do. Your mind, your will, your strength are all connected to the battery of your heart. Keep it charged.
Proverbs 4 v 23

Andrew Robertson

So you want to be a hero?

Of course you do, we all do, although most of us give up on the idea as we grow up and settle for keeping out of the way and getting by. That's not good enough for me though. I want to make a difference, live for something, die for something, beat the bad guy, rescue the damsel in distress and save the world!

And why not? Why not aim high? Trouble is we have a problem. We all want to be heroes but we all inherited 'wimp' genes from Adam, our great, great, great, great, great... grandparent.

Leigh Winsbury

But there is a choice. Because there is a real hero, one who invites you and me to join in a life of living heroically. You see Adam didn't bother defending the girl when the bad guy came along and that cost the earth. But Jesus is different. He lays down His life for His bride, seals the bad guy's doom and saves the world.

But right now, here in the middle of history, all things hang in the balance, waiting for the choices to be made. And right now, right here is you. You trying to make sense of life, trying to see where you fit into it all. Are you a hero or just another bad guy? So far you don't know yourself well enough to find out. A bit of both maybe?

Leigh Winsbury

Well here is how it goes; if you want to be a hero, you need to choose it. If you make no choice, just go with the flow, then nothing will happen. You will make little impact, maybe just settle for being a nice guy. Or you could choose to be another villain. They seem to have all the fun, but then they always come to a sticky end – always!

Leigh Winsbury

> 'Whatever happened to all of the heroes?'
> *No More Heroes*, The Stranglers

Or you could choose Jesus, join a new family and inherit new genes – Jesus genes! When it's in your blood to do it, being heroic comes naturally – no great effort. But be warned, being the hero will be costly in a world where honour and virtue will meet few who value or recognise them.

Life is tough and not fair. That's how it is. The bad guys get away with all sorts and the good guys get laughed at, beat up and ignored. At least until the end of the story when all wrongs are righted; when the King returns to claim His own.

Leigh Winsbury

> A hero is no braver than an ordinary man, but he is braver five minutes longer.
> Ralph Waldo Emerson

> The hero draws inspiration from the virtue of his ancestors.
> Johann Wolfgang Von Goethe

So remember this, we are surrounded by a massive crowd of heroes who have battled to live the life of faith in days gone by, and let us chuck away the stuff that slows us down, especially the toxic, harmful distractions that so easily trip us up. And let us keep running, keep sweating, keep pounding those streets in the race that God has given us to run. How? Find out about Jesus and keep looking to him. Nothing else defines your faith in the same way, no song, no sermon, no preacher, no rock singer, no worship leader, no DVD, no book (not even this one). Get in touch with the one who was willing to die a brutal, bloody, horrible death because of the good things he knew would be his afterwards. And you are one of those good things. He bled and sweated and screamed with agony and poured out his guts for you. And he is now in a place where he can help you. Remember all that when you get tired and depressed and want to give up.

Based on Hebrews 12 vv 1-3

When each of my sons turned 13 I gave them a sword.
Not a little toy job, but a big, real, useable broadsword. Unfortunately I can't give you one as I would like. Giving away swords with books is probably more than publishers can afford, though I bet sales would rocket!

So the swords? Here's why. Seven reasons:

1. Swords are dangerous. So are you. Letting a young man loose on the world could lead to anything. You are a force to be reckoned with and must give account for what you do with who you are.

Leigh Winsbury

When each of my sons turned 13 I gave them a sword. (continued)

2. It's a hidden strength. You can't wave a sword around in public these days, you'd get locked up. You don't need to use it to know it's there – being a man is like that. Jesus is King of the universe but washed His mates' feet and got nailed up for nothing worse than love. He could have called it off at any time, could have but didn't.

3. It's costly – swords don't come cheap and neither does real manhood. Being a real man in a world that doesn't like it will be hard work.

4. It's a weapon. OK so that's obvious but, plainly and simply to remind you that you can fight for what is right, not to remain passive in a world that needs real men to stand up and be counted.

Leigh Winsbury

5. It's cross-shaped – to keep you humble. You are who you are and can be what you can be only because Jesus bought you back from the devil by the price of His own blood – shed on a cross.

6. It's a symbol of the Holy Spirit – let Him and the words He gives you be your strength and defence.

7. To remind you – WE ARE AT WAR! Whether we like it or not, whatever we choose, the war goes on. May as well get on the winning side early. But the fight is in the spirit realm. Look behind the obvious, find the real enemy then strike hard in Jesus name.

Leigh Winsbury

As Joshua approached the city of Jericho, he looked up and saw a man facing him with a sword in his hand. Joshua went up to him and asked, 'Whose side are you on? Are you a friend or an enemy?'

'Neither one,' he replied. 'I am commander of the Lord's army. The real question is - whose side are you on?'

At this, Joshua fell with his face to the ground in reverence. 'I am at your command,' Joshua said. 'What do you want your servant to do?'

The commander of the Lord's army replied, 'Take off your sandals, for this is holy ground.' And Joshua did as he was told.

Joshua 5 vv 13-15

'You think of his sword and your sword and nothing else.'

Hector to his brother Paris as he goes into battle in the movie *Troy*

Love is patient and kind. It does not push others down or beat them up. It is not proud and arrogant. Not foul-mouthed or stupidly ignorant. Love respects all and looks for the best in others. It doesn't give up. Ever. 1 Corinthians 13

> It's easy to think God made things to be loved and people to be used. Instead of the other way round.

'Somewhere between our things and our stuff is the real us.' From the movie *Bobby*

> 'Life is what happens to you while you're making plans.' John Lennon

Never stop playing.

'We don't stop playing because we grow old, we grow old because we stop playing.'
George Bernard Shaw

Jesus knew his mates had been arguing about who was the greatest, the funniest, the best looking, the cleverest, the strongest, so he brought a little child to his side. Then he said to them, 'Look at this little girl. She isn't considered powerful or successful or perfect. But she is curious, honest, silly, stubborn, straightforward and funny. Anyone who welcomes a little child like this on my behalf welcomes me, and anyone who welcomes me welcomes my Father who sent me. God's ways are often found in the crazy places. The uncool places. Take note. Don't be like everyone else, be different. If you want to be great in God's eyes then take the world's ways with a pinch of salt. Learn what it means to be humble, kind and caring.' Luke 9 vv 46&47

Dear Son,
When I was at school.
When I was only fifteen.
One of my teachers asked the class a question.'
'What do you want to do with your life? Would you like to be happy?
Or would you like to change the world?'
Slowly, tentatively, each of us put our hands up.
Half of the class wanted to be happy.
And the other half wanted to do something that would make the world a better place.
Thirty years have passed.

Anonymous

Thirty years and more.
And I've watched my classmates.
And my friends.
And my family.
And my workmates.
And I've finally figured it out.
Only just figured it out.
Those weren't two answers.
Not two answers at all.
No, those answers were one and the same.
Maybe that's why Jesus said, 'Whoever finds his life will lose it, and whoever loses his life for my sake will find it.'

Anonymous

> Jesus told some great stories, in fact he told them all the time. He didn't do sermons, he told funny, shocking, memorable stories. The kind you'd forward to your friends, or retweet on your phone. And tucked away in each one was a secret, a secret about the ways of God.
> Matthew 13 v 34

Let those who are wise listen to these proverbs and become even wiser. And let those who understand receive guidance by exploring the depth of meaning in these proverbs, parables, wise sayings and riddles. Proverbs 1 vv 5&6

> Keep asking, looking, hammering on those doors. Don't sit back, beat on the windows of heaven.
> The kingdom is closer than you think.

Why read to our boys?

Why read to our boys? Why read with them? It leaves a lasting legacy, that's why.

I was reminded of this not long ago when I was chatting with my son, who is now nearly 30.

We were talking about some of the books we had read together as a family, and Madeleine L'Engle's beautiful *Wrinkle in Time* series came up.

'Do you remember the time we read it out loud in the restaurant?' he asked. 'We were reading the books at dinner time at home and we were in the middle of one of them, so we carried on when we went out to dinner that night.'

I have to be honest - I remembered that we'd read the series. Sadly, however, I'd fogotten that particular night. But he hadn't. He hadn't. It had stuck with him as a special memory. And that's what we want to leave our boys. Those memories - of us and books and them together.

Anonymous

> We males are scared of plenty of things, yet we seem to spend much of our time trying to look as if we're afraid of nothing.

> It is part of being a healthy human being to hope, dream, trust, trip up, get tempted, cry, laugh, fail, succeed, fall down, get injured, have our hearts broken, care, believe, doubt and get confused.

The spirit of God inspires all good things. A guy called Bezalel in the Bible was a great craftsman, a skilled designer and a wise teacher. Because he was full of God's Holy Spirit. Exodus 35 vv 30-35

With God in your life you start producing a few useful things. Like compassion for other people, happiness about the good things, and a desire to spread peace. God can help you be more patient and caring, sticking by others and more in control of your anger and passion. Galatians 5 vv 22&23

> 'If you ask God for patience do you think God gives you patience? Or does he give you situations where you can learn to be patient?'
> From the movie *Evan Almighty*

'I find bantering with other guys really hard. The competition to be the wittiest and coolest is tough. I always end up feeling an idiot and excluded from the conversation. I feel a failure.'

> Jesus asked his mates what they'd been bantering about on the road, but they didn't want to say because they'd been arguing about which one was the greatest/coolest/funniest/strongest.
> Mark 9 vv 33&34

Lots of people look for success,
and certainly I can't remember anyone at school who wanted to be a failure! However we're human beings, not human doings, and our value is not linked simply to the success of projects or ventures we work with.

Fruitfulness is a better, more subtle measure. It has a great deal to do with character. In a world of instant drinks and constant online connections, we are tempted to look for instant results in relationships and our own personal lives. You may feel like the years have already shot past and others are racing ahead of you, but living well is more of a marathon than a sprint. So dream big dreams that stir hearts and minds, but also take time out, keep a journal, make sure you have those who will mentor you, keep yourself accountable.

Luke Walton

I've heard that the Chinese have a saying

'For a year plant grain; for a decade plant trees; for a century plant people'. Long-term fruitfulness is about people, so work at relationships and integrity with humility. Build steadily towards your audacious vision with patient commitment and courage. Trust God and take risks!

Luke's account of Jesus Baptism tells us that a voice from heaven declared 'you are my son in whom I'm well pleased'. If I could offer you any gift at all, it would be that you too would know that God delights over you. He delights in the person you are, not the person you think you should be, or might become. The question then is how well do you know what it is he delights in? There are lots of systems that can offer you the chance to learn more about your character, gifts and skills and if you have never looked at one of these you should do so now!

Luke Walton

Hospitality is a fantastic gift.
If you haven't already,
learn to cook now.

Luke Walton

> 'I'm here knocking on the door. If you open the door to me I'll come in and we'll have a great meal together. We'll get to know each other and share our lives.' Revelation 3 v 21

When Matthew started following Jesus the first thing he did was throw a big party and invite all his friends. Matthew 9 vv 9&10

For many years I remembered one teacher above all others – Nigel Bates. He taught me Geography, but also offered wisdom that counts, a passion about world justice and was just great fun. When I eventually got around to writing and thanking him it turned out that the letter arrived at a time that had been very tough for him. So is there someone you haven't thanked? A teacher, a leader, a family member or a friend? Write to them now and thank them, you have no idea the impact that could have.

Luke Walton

> 'No one forgets a good teacher.'

// Men 37 Boys //

I am the father of 2 sons now in their early 30's, both married, and the older of whom is himself a father now.

Some years ago, when they were in their late teens I attended a conference, during which one of the speakers said he had recently learned an important lesson in relation to his teenage son. He'd realised that while he'd often told him how proud he was of him and his achievements, - and incidentally do we dads even do that enough? – but what he hadn't done for years, was simply tell him that he loved him.

This acknowledgement immediately hit home to me, and made me ask myself when I had last told my 2 sons that I loved them. Like the speaker I certainly told them I was proud of them, but for whatever reason – not very 'macho', feeling self-conscious, not wanting to embarrass them, - I hadn't actually come out with those three little words.

Rt. Revd. Chris Edmondson
Bishop of Bolton

When an opportunity presented itself after I returned from the conference, I put right this omission, and while – 16 years on – I by no means say it every time I see them, nonetheless I am so glad of that speaker back in 1997 who challenged me to 'come right out and say it' – 'I love you'.

All of which is consistent with Jesus' own experience at his Baptism, where he heard the words from his heavenly Father: 'you are my son, whom I love, with whom I am well pleased.' Love expressed in terms of identity, security and affirmation – and bear in mind, Jesus hadn't actually 'done' anything in terms of ministry at this point!

> And a voice came from Heaven, 'You are my Son, whom I love; with you I am well pleased.'
> Luke 3 v 22

Rt. Revd. Chris Edmondson
Bishop of Bolton

> 'Car manufacturers don't name their cars after what men are really like – the Ford Clumsy, the Nissan Moody, you won't find these vehicles.'
> Bill Bailey

You are more than the shoes on your feet, more than the clothes you buy. More than the music you listen to, the movies you watch, the jokes you tell, the food you eat, the people you date, the exams you pass. You are the image of God, valued by the one who designed you, cared for by him. That's what makes you – You.

At High School, we had a bully of a teacher
who was nicknamed Big Bill.
He stank of stale sweat and cheap aftershave and had been known, when corporal punishment was allowed, to physically strap sixth form girls. Everybody was scared of him. Nobody dared to speak in his class and when he made even a mild joke, we all roared with laughter to get in his good books. I used to wonder why people like him were so malevolent.

One day I got talking to a boy in my year who lived round the corner from Big Bill. He never had Bill as a teacher, so he hadn't suffered like some of us. He (Andrew) told me that in his own house Bill was as quiet as a mouse. He was dominated by his wife and couldn't control his daughter who, on one occasion, had covered her father's suede shoes in green gloss paint.

John

After that I realised that bullies sometimes bully because they have been bullied or seen through, and they then try to take it out on others. It doesn't excuse him, but ever since I've sometimes felt sympathy for people who are vile to others because they don't feel happy in themselves.

John

'If a child lives with approval, he learns to live with himself.' Dorothy Law Nolte

The Tom-tom of Life

Sometimes as we drive the roads of life, we find ourselves reliant on The Tom-tom of Life (or... The Tw*t Nav as my mate Johnny Husband refers to it.) I was just pootling along, thought I was doing well. I'd been concentrating on getting good lines through the corners, avoiding obstacles on the journey, trying not to use too much fuel, following the TN's instructions to the letter. [I thought?!] Seeing places I thought I recognised, and I genuinely thought I had everything under control. Then I turn round the bend to a total dead end in progress. I'm going too fast, the conditions are not what they were and things have become suddenly treacherous. To the orchestral accompaniment of rubber on tarmac and folding metal I come to a sudden stop. Another bloody 'car crash' and not something I can just turn round from but something I need to extricate myself from with the minimum of further damage possible.

Chris Hutchison

Once again I find myself muttering the familiar mantras: 'How the Frappuccino did I end up here?' And of course... 'HEEELP!!!!'

I mean, really I knew that this place/stuff existed/happened. And looking back there was some indication that this was indeed a wrong turn but instead of listening to my quiet inner voice and natural sense of direction I carried on with the music blaring and the TN bleating, holding my phone to my ear. 'La la la, not listening!' Window down, elbow out, giving the customary thumb and forefinger O shaped wave to anyone I figured deserved it, and generally looking rather cool if I say so myself. Till, as already mentioned, screech... bang... 'What the frap! How did I get here... Again!?!?!?'

Chris Hutchison

It's at this point I find I have a choice! Do I keep up all the distractions, do a rubbish 15 point turn/about face, pretend like nothing happened, hope no one noticed and try my best to retrace my steps. Or do I look my mistakes in the eye? Try my best to learn enough to keep me out of this or that 'car crash' once and for all?

My mate Dave would cite the mighty Billy Joel as one of my greatest musical influences and he'd be right. Billy wrote a song called *We're only human* some millennia ago which stated that we're supposed to make mistakes and he furnished me with a line or philosophy for life, probably not his line but he knew it before me and these things are passed onto us from all walks or 'drives' of life...

'You're mistakes are the only things you can truly call your own'. I believe he's right!

Chris Hutchison

I continue to be distracted, to lose my way, to revisit the same sh*tty stuff... time and time again sometimes. But not every time. On occasions I do stick to a prescribed route because I know it's the best way.

Another buddy of mine from work says very wisely, 'You can't cherry pick from life!' You make your choice and sometimes it comes good, sometimes not. We all make choices good and bad and that's how it's supposed to be. The important thing is that we use it all to inform and guide our present, which was our future and is our past.

Chris Hutchison

Don't worry

I would say one thing to people; don't worry! Don't worry about where you are going in life, don't worry about ambition, don't worry about the way you look; in short, don't worry!!! This sounds naïve but it isn't; all worrying seems to do is make us anxious and uncertain of everything. I've learnt that before everything, we should have a simple but strong faith in God; nothing more, nothing less!

Tim Childs

Don't worry (continued)
Here are God's words on the matter: 'Then he said to his disciples, 'That is why I am telling you not to worry about your life and what you are to eat, nor about your body and how you are to clothe it. For life is more than food, and the body more than clothing. Think of the ravens. They do not sow or reap; they have no storehouses and no barns; yet God feeds them. And how much more you are worth than the birds! Can any of you, however much you worry, add a single cubit to your span of life? If a very small thing is beyond your powers, why worry about the rest?' (Luke 12:22-26 NJB) Learn to put all your worries, concerns, hopes, fears and ambitions in prayer to God.

Tim Childs

Jesus, our Best Mate

In life we're all looking for that one person that won't let us down, the one person who is always there for us, who is never sick and tired of us; that's a tall order these days when everyone is so busy, busy on Facebook or Twitter or busy texting their mates to tell them they've just reached the bus stop, or busy texting their mates that they'll be busy texting another mate! No one seems to have much time for anyone these days; we're all so busy!

Jesus is our best mate, a true friend who knows all about us and wants to give us a better life and bring us an abundant life, regardless of who we are and what we have or haven't done. Jesus accepts us as who we are, uncultured and unrefined and rough around the edges though we might be; Jesus accepts Jack-the-Lads as much as He accepts holier-than-thou types; He is always an 'equal-opportunities' Messiah!

Tim Childs

Religion or Christianity?

Many people like myself find 'traditional' Christianity completely uninspiring; singing merry hymns on Sunday in some suburban church and saying hello to the Vicar just doesn't hold much appeal. It doesn't reach out to me, it doesn't speak of an all-mighty but unfathomable God, it speaks to me of assured social status, a church for those who've got it all together, a religion for the terminally nice.

Not being a bloke with it all together, I truly wonder how I would be treated in such a place. Would I be accepted? And isn't that the crux of all human uncertainty; whether we are accepted by other people or not? People may not accept us, for many reasons, but we have a Saviour who not only accepts us though we might be low-born, but actually chooses us in many cases because we are outcasts and downcast and not important in the eyes of the world.

Tim Childs

A study revealed that although we can look back at our lives 10 years ago and recognise the huge changes that have taken place, as we get older we find it increasingly difficult to believe that will happen again. Most people are poor at developing a vision and a plan for the next 10 years despite huge potential for change and growth. Isaiah's encouragement to wait on God whatever our age springs to mind.
Isaiah 40 vv 27-31

Luke Walton

What have you been designed for?
What do you do best?
What inspires you?
What can you do, however small or big, which might enrich the lives of others?

'God made me fast, and when I run I feel his pleasure.' Eric Liddell, in the film *Chariots of Fire*

Heroes & villains in the Bible

Abraham the liar
Jacob the cheat
Moses the murderer
Joseph the cocky guy
Samson the spoilt brat
David the killer and adulterer
Peter the fool
Thomas the doubting guy
Nicodemus the coward
Paul the bully

In spite of their mistakes, crimes and misdemeanours they all went down in history as guys who did their best to serve God amongst their mess.

> **In Jesus everyone is the same.**
> There are no divisions or discriminations. Whatever colour, background, nationality, sex, preference, personality, experience. We can all come to God as we are. He is the great leveller.
> Galatians 3 v 28

In their song *The Living Years*

Mike and the Mechanics send out the call to keep communicating. Not least with our fathers, and maybe with the other men we know too.

'I wasn't there that morning when my Father passed away.
I didn't get to tell him all the things I had to say.
I just wish I could have told him in the living years.'

> **Football was invented because men have got nothing to say to their mates.**
> Ben Elton

We need to get real with each other and stop covering over the cracks with our English barriers. I must admit, though, there is a fine line between being honest and becoming a constant whinger. We will have to find the balance somewhere.

Get real, get some good mates who you can be honest with AND who ask you tough questions.
It's worth it in the long run, I know from experience.

Lee from leeandbaz.com

Beyond the banter!

To move towards good relationships with people, we need to develop a greater sense of honesty and realness. I used to work at the Crown Court in Leeds (I thought I'd start as a criminal and work my way up!). As an admin officer, I shuffled paper from one side of my desk to the other and then went home. In the mornings there used to be a ritual that drove me mad: it was the 'say hello to everyone' game. Everyone used to say, 'Hello, good morning, how are you?' but no one ever replied honestly or ever listened for a reply! 'Yeah, fine thanks', 'Not bad' or 'Fair to middling' were the only responses. Some people even answered the question when you hadn't asked them! I loved giving people more information than they wanted: 'Well, I feel a bit tired, actually, and I'm concerned about my relationship with my wife, and my dog has fleas.' You have never seen people run so fast.

Lee from leeandbaz.com

For us blokes, the depth issue is easy to push further — try steering conversations away from football, cars and 'what I would do if I won the lottery', and see what happens. Beyond the banter and football talk there is often a man who is lonely and craves true friendship. I know that from my own life. I still have occasional feelings of loneliness and these feelings are shared by some of my (honest) friends. Is the Internet so popular with men because you only share the bits you want to share in selective Facebook-type relationships?

There's life beyond the banter!

Lee from leeandbaz.com

TEH PRONS!

It's everywhere! And you look at it. And its only you. And God hates you for it.

None of the above is true. I would guess 95% of the Christian male population has struggled with porn in one form or another in their life. You are not alone. You are not disgusting. God does not hate you.

God loves you with all his heart. He may not like the things you do (in my case that may be a lot of things) but he loves **you**. God can still use you as you are. God can still speak to you as you are. God wants you to be whole and free to be the person He made you to be.

Ben Price

The biggest way you can combat it is to talk to someone. I don't mean anyone and probably no one you're related to, but someone you trust and who knows Jesus. They may not be able to help BUT being accountable is a step towards being rid of the devil's favourite weapon against you.

There are no formulas to use to combat this as there are often real deep reasons why this is a big issue for so many guys (and girls) and I'd encourage you to seek wise prayerful people and start to explore this. Like any addiction the first battle is to admit you have a problem and resolve to do something about it. Keep on fighting. Keep on getting up and going on. You **can** be free. Never believe the lie that you won't be.

Ben Price

Life is hard.
It's simple and it's a fact. If you think others have it easy and you must be doing something wrong, don't. Jesus never promised us an easy life either BUT he did promise he'd be with us all the way and that we wouldn't have to face the hard life alone.

God made you to be the unique, wonderful person you are. Why would he want to suppress your given talents and abilities? Why feel the need to pray 'Lord may the words I speak be your words and not mine' when he's made you with an intellect and soul that's bursting with promise?

Ben Price

Keep seeking the Glory of God.
That's not to glorify God but to be in the presence of God; to seek to always be in His presence. Speak to the sleeping parts of your heart. Awaken the parts that yawn at Bible study, or are lethargic about worship. This is not about you trying to do it yourself but about allowing God to meet you in those sleeping places and fire your heart into action.

Think upon this: Love. It's not a cute fluffy pink thing that girls like. It's not chocolates, hearts and flowers. Its not seedy pictures pinned up on lockers. Its not hippies with rainbow braces. Its the stuff that the universe craves. It's the very essence of a huge and powerful God. It's the answer to deep personal questions. It is rugged and tough. It survives death, famine and war. It is life in all its fullness.

Ben Price

It's worth asking why guys look at sexualised images. It's probably because we are affected by what we see. Advertisers use this all the time.

It's also worth remembering that when we make mistakes God invites us to run towards him, not away from him. We don't have to hide the bad, embarrassing, damaging things we do from him.

> 'I was born a sinner, I have always been that sort of person. And you know that. I'm only human. What you want is for me to be honest about that, so that you can help me get my head together and face up to myself. The truth can set me free. Clean me up God, give me a new start. Wash away the crap and forgive me please.'
> Psalm 51 vv 5-7

So you are in your teens.
And in a few years you'll be grown up! Aggggh!

Don't waste a minute it's a great road, full of challenges and an exciting adventure.
When you look back from your 40s... you'll not believe where the time has gone, and you may wonder why you still feel like a teenager! (We never really grow up, cos we're only boys really!) You'll regret doing some things, but don't hold those regrets, they really are a waste of time. In those years you did stuff to excite, and explore, but often just to use up spare time and with the internet it became easier just to look at things. You probably thought it was exciting, but it was actually polluting. Believe me porn has rotted you from the inside out, and it will take real love, faith and trust to work it out.

Dave Hase

Soar on wings like eagles

The first Bible passage that connected with me before I even thought I was a follower of Jesus was Isaiah 40:

The Lord is the everlasting God, the Creator of the ends of the earth.

He will not grow tired or weary, and his understanding no one can fathom.

He gives strength to the weary and increases the power of the weak.

Even youths grow tired and weary, and young men stumble and fall;

but those who hope in the Lord will renew their strength.

They will soar on wings like eagles; they will run and not grow weary, they will walk and not be faint.

Dave Hase

I love eagles and their freedom,
but more importantly 'wings like eagles' caught my attention because it was the title of a book my wife gave me about a pilot who used to fly helicopters for the Army in Northern Ireland. And then, because he was a Christian, started doing amazing things for people by flying into difficult places around the world with Mission Aviation Fellowship. It was the first time I saw that this faith had meaning in real stuff being done for the benefit of others. I know there is loads more to the Isaiah passage, but that is what first got to me.

Dave Hase

Ride out to defend truth, humility, justice.
God's throne endures forever, and his power is expressed through justice. He loves what is right and hates what is corrupt.
Psalm 45 vv 3-7

> For evil to prosper good men just need to do nothing.

Wanted: Men who understand the times and know what action to take. Men who see things clearly and know what to do.
1 Chronicles 12 v 32

How did Jesus relate to men?

Some thoughts taken from Mark chapters 1-9.

He offered them a job.
Invited them to 'Follow me'. Men follow men.
Gave them nicknames - Rocky, the Thunder Boys.
Trusted them and gave them responsibility - sent them out on his behalf.
Took them travelling.
Went home and ate with them.
Allowed them to break Sabbath laws.
Made use of their working skills - sailing and fishing.
Commissioned them with tasks and power.
Told them stories about workers.
Told them they were part of something – he gave them the secrets of his kingdom.
Used men as key characters in his parables.

How did Jesus relate to men (continued)?

He showed his power in the context of their lives – boats, storms, work, parties, home life.
Used their boats to travel.
Taught by example.
Sent them off with short sharp instructions. Made it risky and challenging. Told them to take minimum luggage. (Great news if you've ever had to pack a car for a family holiday.)
Gave them the chance to debrief and listened to their stories.
Took them off for some R & R.
Involved them practically - made them help out with feeding 5000 people.
Sent them off on a difficult journey at night.
He was honest about his hopes and fears.
Showed them astonishing glimpses of God's power.

Following Jesus is not so much about becoming more spiritual, but becoming more human. More the men God made us to be. It's about realising he is right there in the everyday moments, already part of ordinary and extraordinary life. Our personality, experiences, mistakes and triumphs, our strengths and weaknesses can all be offered to him and used by him.
Nothing is wasted. He understands totally what it is to be a man.

> 'The glory of God is a human being fully alive.'
> St Irenaeus

The men in the Bible

are very different to one another. Samson is brash and loud, Boaz is quiet and thoughtful. Joshua is a military genius, Moses is a mystical shepherd. David is a mood swing, guitar playing, rock'n'roll poet kind of king. His son Solomon is a loose cannon with the ladies. Nimrod is the first action hero. Jonah is a reluctant adventurer. Luke is a studious, careful writer. Paul is a tough talking, pedantic teacher.

There's room for all of us in this thing.

Without vision people perish. With no purpose in life people can curl up, fade away and die.
I often want to just sit on the sofa with a cheeseburger going nowhere. If we aim for nothing we will probably hit it.
Proverbs 29 v 18

This is what God asks of men – to live true lives of justice, kindness and humility. This is worship, this is discipleship, this is following Jesus. Trudging along in the footsteps of the man of justice, kindness and humility.
Micah 6 v 8

> 'I get knocked down, but I get up again, ain't nothing gonna keep me down.'
> *Tubthumpin'*, Chumbawumba

You are everywhere God. You're not afraid of the dark and you love the light. Wherever I go you are there. Even if the place feels difficult, depressing or dangerous. You can see in the dark and the sun won't blind you. Majestic or bleak, no place is beyond your reach.
Psalm 139 vv 7-12

> 'Have the courage to live. Anyone can die.'
> Robert Cody

'Children enjoy the present because they have neither a past nor a future.'
Jean de la Bruyere

God is intensely interested
in those who love and respect him. His kindness towards us is as massive as the universe. He has removed our rebellious acts further away from us than the North Pole is from the South. He threw them away and they just kept going.

> Imagine a good father, a kind, patient, cheerful, enthusiastic dad. That's what God is like. Watching his children, listening to them, seeing even the smallest good things we do. He knows how weak we are, he understands the human condition. He knows how we are wired up.
> And he loves us all the same.
> Psalm 103 vv 11-14

Music in my life

Picture this: a young child, probably no more than three years old, just beginning to stir from sleep on a Sunday morning. And the first sounds that fill his heart, mind and spirit, are the sounds of a piano. Played softly, hauntingly... well known hymns with strange, poignant harmonies... beautiful, stirring chords to support the familiar melodies. There is comfort here - this is the sound that always accompanies the first moments of Sunday morning, safe, home, the little boy...

and Father.

> 'Every child is an artist. The problem is how to remain an artist once he grows up.'
> Pablo Picasso

Adrian Snell

The young boy is me, Adrian. The father is my father. And to this day I can hear this outpouring of my father's heart. He loved the classic hymns - as I did and still do. But he played them his way, with his harmonies. He could not read notes, but his playing by ear was totally fluent and had a depth and melancholy that, even to a three year old, was clearly his heartsong.

Later in life, long into my own journey as a composer, I shared these memories with my father, and remarked that I was always drawn to the 'black' keys - particularly G flat! 'That was my key too,' he replied, 'G flat with its beautiful patterns, haunting colour, and ease of moving chord to chord.' It was as if I'd inherited his key as well as his freckles and fat fingers!

Adrian Snell

From those early, formative memories, how do I begin to tell the story of music in my life? For I cannot remember a single moment of my life when music has not, in some way or another, been the 'language of my heart'. How many times have I used that phrase when speaking to others? And how many times have I used the words, first penned by the biblical psalmist, 'deep calls to deep' when trying to throw more light upon this mystical, deeply emotional and spiritual act of communication between music and the heart.

I have wept, prayed, cried out, danced, laughed, screamed, lost and found life, raged, demanded answers, asked impossible questions and refused to give or receive easy answers... all in song, and in songs without words. Music is breath to me - more than a friend, and yet, just as often a stranger... dark, unknown... frightening even. Where will it take me - as a listener, and as a writer?

Adrian Snell

My very identity is caught up in music.
The music that I play and listen to tells me who I am… and others if they have ears to hear. And if they don't… then I can be utterly alone and lonely too.

Never have I felt so complete and alive as those moments when a performance communicated - completely - to the audience. When they understood and responded with one heart somehow.

> 'I think music, in itself, is healing. It's an explosive expression of humanity. It's something we are all touched by. No matter what culture we're from, everyone loves music.' Billy Joel

Adrian Snell

Never was there such intimacy
as the act of making music with another - improvised, unexpected, heart to heart. An unspoken act of union through sound, witnessed by no-one else, without the need to analyse or dissect - just an unrepeatable moment, yet a moment of total confirmation that this language of the heart and soul transcends all and was meant to.

> 'Without music, life is a journey through a desert.' Pat Conroy

What words could ever express enough gratitude to the Creator of this universe who, having formed man and woman out of the dust of the earth, should create within them the desire, the hunger to explore sound, use hands, voice and breath to organise, disorganise, experiment, invent? But then we were made in His Image. Imagine the music of God!

Adrian Snell

Jesus was a baby,
a toddler, a boy, a teenager, a young guy, a working man. A builder and carpenter, a man who ran his own business. A man who faced recession and high taxes, who lived under the oppression of an invading Roman army. He had tough times with his family, was rejected for a while. He had enemies and friends, rivals and supporters. He knows what life is like.

Jesus taught about trouble, anger, lust, relationships, language, revenge, money, sex, temptation, respect, humility, greed, power, bullying, generosity, compassion, practical caring, justice, poor, risk, faith, doubt, honesty, worship, forgiveness, compassion, giving , praying, fasting, attitudes, worry, criticising, persisting and being productive. He lived what he taught. He walked his talk.

You can check this out in Matthew 5 & 6.

Emails

Recently I came across the true story of the father who emailed his children to tell them they were a disappointment to him. He had built up a reserve of resentment and suddenly let the dam burst in one blood-curdling, critical message.

On the flip side, this is God's email to us:
I knew you before I formed you in your mother's womb. Before you were born I chose you.
Do not be afraid, for I have put my life on the line for you. I know you by name; you are mine. When you go through troubles, I will be with you. When you go through rivers of difficulty, you will not drown. When you walk through the fire of temptation and oppression, you will not be burned up. For I am the Lord, your God, your rescuer and leader. I gave my son to buy your freedom. I traded his life for yours because you are precious to me. You are respected by me, and I love you.
Jeremiah 1 vv 4&5 and Isaiah 43 vv 1-4

Incarnation
My Dad died suddenly when I was 21. I dreamt about him every night for a year after that, as my subconscious wrestled to come to terms with this new reality. The intervening years have been punctuated with moments of acute awareness of following in his footsteps - the obvious things, like marriage; raising children; making, keeping and losing friends; and taking on a public role in the life of the Church.

Stuart Townend

And the less obvious, the things I never saw, but know he must have gone through too: the burden of domestic responsibilities; the disappointments, the temptations, the self-doubt that accompany private life and public ministry; and the growing awareness of the ticking clock on your own mortality.

I'm sad that I never got the chance to talk though these things with him as an adult. But it's in this process of walking his road, and seeing him in me in so many ways, that I feel I know him more intimately than any conversation could reveal.

Stuart Townend

Email from a Friend

How are you? Just wanted to send you a message to see how you're doing and let you know I'm thinking about you. I saw you yesterday as you were talking with your friends, then later as you were walking home alone. I waited all day hoping you might take a moment to talk to me too. In the evening I gave you a clear sky to close your day, and a warm breeze to encourage you outside. I'm sorry you didn't come. It bothered me, but of course it doesn't affect the way I feel about you.

I watched you toss and turn last night, and I longed to reach down and calm your fears. I spilled some moonlight across your face, something to dispel the darkness. I was hoping we might talk then and you did say one or two things as you finally dozed off to sleep. You woke late this morning, and had to rush off out of the house. We missed each other again.

There were moments today when you looked so sad and alone. I can barely stand to watch sometimes. I do understand your pain and frustration, believe me. People let me down all the time, they push me aside, ridicule me, and act as if I don't exist. But it doesn't quench the passion I have.

I try to tell you about it in the majesty of the mist-covered mountains, in the spectacular surf as it rolls and breaks across the bay, in the power of the midnight thunder and the heat of the noonday sun. I whisper to you in the rustle of the crickets and grasshoppers, and I shout to you in the rushing rivers and roaring fires. I fill the air with the guitar riffs of nature and the call of the wild, and every scent, every sound is there to remind you – I care – and I'll never stop.

Email from a Friend (continued)
How can I help you see it? How can I help you know I'll never give up on you? Everyone else can see that I value and respect you – but it's so hard for you to see it for yourself.

I've been wondering about that. Perhaps if I send my son to show you. Perhaps if he steps into the dust that lies across your path, puts his feet in your shoes, walks the road you have to walk, and feels the tortured pain you often feel, perhaps if you could hear him laughing at the jokes you enjoy.

Then I remind myself, he's already done that once, already been there and experienced what you experience. Seen the things you see, thought the things you think and felt the emotions you feel.

Please never stop looking to me, I miss you when we don't stay in touch. Don't give up.
And whatever you do, don't forget about me.

A few thoughts

So here's what I want you to do, and God will help you as you do it: Take your everyday, ordinary life - the moments of your sleeping, eating, working, chatting, struggling, laughing, thinking, listening. Take it all and place it before God as an offering. Embrace what God has given you and what he does for you - that's the best thing you can do for him. This is being spiritual, this is worship, this will make God smile.

Don't become so well-adjusted to your culture that you fit into it without even thinking. Don't be moulded by the adverts and rumours and peer pressure. Instead, fix your attention on God. Let your thinking be freshened up by him. Find out what he wants and do your best to get it for him. You'll be changed then from the inside out. God will bring the best out of you, and you will grow and develop and become mature in him.
Romans 12 vv 1-2

I still remember the chemistry lesson when as a young teenager I was offered an image of our world made up of atoms, comprised of a nucleus and electrons, and combined together into compounds. Somehow, on that particular afternoon, I had a glimpse of the awesome beauty in our world. I've had it again since, looking into a microscope and up at the clear night sky. I love the beauty of the world and the way that science draws me closer to God through his incredible creativity.

Justin Tomkins

Doesn't the world change fast?
I was stopped in my tracks six years ago now when I read some ideas about how the world will have changed out of all recognition within another three decades. I don't know what the future will look like but I'm committed to being prepared to expect change. I know each generation has faced their own challenges but no previous generation has had to engage with the rapid developments in science, medicine and technology we are presented with today. I pray that we will hold on fast to what it means to be human in this context of change.

Justin Tomkins

I love the philosophy of 'life's too short to...' said, and more importantly embodied, with such passion and energy by a relative of mine. He's not prepared to waste a day in unnecessary regret or unhelpful analysis of the past. He'll reflect on life, for sure, but nothing stops him appreciating the moment. He savours food, takes in every bit of beauty around him, notices every bit of wildlife and relishes each new encounter with a stranger. In doing so, he seems to learn so much and enjoy so much. I find his love of life infectious.

Justin Tomkins

My grandfather's generosity is an inspiration. During his childhood, his service in the Second World War, and his raising of a family in post-war England he developed a self-discipline which enables him to exercise such incredible self-control. For as long as I've known him he's so careful about what he uses for himself, monitoring his use of water, his food, and what he spends upon himself. Yet, he pours out generosity upon others. I pray for peace yet I also pray that, in the absence of war, my children and I might learn that same self-control which he demonstrates and might learn his generosity too.

Justin Tomkins

My Dad had such a wonderful gift of making people laugh. Often it would involve teasing one of us, but always in such a way that we were built up. I have never seen anyone else quite so able to put people at ease. He worked as a tailor when he was younger and I remember him telling me how he'd get a customer to exhale before measuring them for trousers, in order to get them to reveal the true size of their waist. He had the same ability to get people to be themselves through his sense of humour. We'd find ourselves letting our guards down and being drawn into community with each other.

Justin Tomkins

There was a wonderful Australian priest
I worked with some years ago now who talked about the difference between thinking of himself as a person and as an individual. When he thought of himself as an individual he thought of what separated him from others, things like his own skin and his location in space. When he thought of himself as a person he thought of all those things which connected him to others, his thoughts and feelings of others, what he'd learned from them, and the memories and ideas of him held in the minds of others, all over the globe; as well as his relationships with others, those still alive, and those already dead. I love that sense of being defined not by what separates me from others, but by what connects me to them.

Justin Tomkins

Ten Commandments for the Under Twenties

1. Thou shalt hold fast the truth that thy life has value and purpose.

2. Thou shalt not make unto thyself any graven image of pop star, TV soap character, or charismatic church leader nor bow down and worship them.

3. Thou shalt be thine own fashion guru.

4. Thou shalt put into life more than thou hopest to take out.

5. Thou shalt not consider anyone over 30 as having one foot in the grave.

Derek Wilson

6. Thou shalt give equal weight to thine own genius and other people's criticisms.

7. Thou shalt not allow thine enthusiasm to be ground down by disappointments or failures.

8. Thou shalt be more concerned to be true to what thou believest than to be popular.

9. Thou shalt make a point of discovering the difference between love and sexual gratification.

10. Thou shalt look forward to all that life has in store and not regard growing older as being an unmitigated disaster.

Derek Wilson

One day you will be middle aged.
The question is, what will you have achieved when you get to my age? More importantly, what kind of man will you be?

Most of the time I'm pretty comfortable in my own skin, but it hasn't always been this way. I like things about my younger self – open, honest, optimistic and single minded. On the other hand I had a pretty poor self-image, didn't really feel fully accepted, and over compensated for this by being uncompromising about my faith. Someone once said, 'a man filled with God cannot be set aside'. I didn't want to be set aside. I wanted my life to count. I wanted to be a great man of God. But in the process I became inflexible in my thinking, unable to live life to the full and occasionally ungracious to others.

Ray - Pubchurch@aol.com

So here's my advice.
It's a quote from the film *Chocolat*:

> 'I think we can't go around measuring our goodness by what we *don't* do. By what we deny ourselves, what we resist and who we exclude. I think we've got to measure goodness by what we embrace, what we create and who we include.'

Ray - Pubchurch@aol.com

Dear Son,

Your Mum and I couldn't be prouder of you. We've been through some 'hairy' times together over the years but we want you to know we love you with all our hearts and always will.

But, if there were one pearl of wisdom that I would like to share with you it would be this: Who you are is way more important than what you do. What Jesus' Father said of Him at His baptism (before Jesus had ever done or said anything in terms of a 'job') is also true of you. 'You are my Son, whom I love; with you I am well pleased.' (Luke 3 v 22) – or as I like to put it, 'You are the son the Father always wanted.'
You have been loved and cherished from all eternity (Ephesians 1 vv 4,5).

John Walker

You are significant because
you were conceived in your Heavenly Father's mind in eternity past to be brought through Jesus into the circle of His love. You are included, you belong, and your Father delights in you. As you well know I'm an orphan – but it is this truth, of being my Father's son, which I have only come to really understand and appreciate way into my adult life which encourages and sustains me every day. I'm my Father's beloved boy, always have been always will be.

And Son – what is true of you and me is also true of everyone else you see around you. Look on them as being eternally loved and encourage them to share in our Father's love together.

All my love,

Your Dad and Brother

John Walker

Learn how to say sorry –
but not so quickly that you miss working through the circumstances which led to your saying or doing what you did. Give the person(s) you hurt time and space to share how your words or actions affected them – and then genuinely apologize.

Learn how to forgive - but not so quickly that you miss working through the circumstances surrounding the hurt you suffered. Give the person(s) who hurt you the time and space to share how their words or actions affected you (or at least try and put yourself in their shoes) – and then genuinely forgive.

John Walker

> I once heard Bishop David Sheppard (former England cricketer and Anglican Bishop) say: 'If at first you don't succeed, ask yourself why.'

Remember as you grow up that you have a whole life's journey ahead of you. Your cherished beliefs now may (will) adapt and change as you grow older. Be humble and patient with those who believe or express their faith differently from you. You may have something to learn from them. There's some truth in the maxim: 'Until you're grey you have nothing to say!'

> There is no shame in having the courage to change your mind.

John Walker

When the time comes for you to get married Son – remember what your Mum says to me: 'Happy Wife, Happy Life!'

> The people I have most admired in my life-long Christian pilgrimage are those who have become more loving and inclusive as they have grown older.

Have the courage to wait. Delayed gratification often has a sweet taste.

When it comes to thinking which church to 'belong' to – don't forget that 'small is beautiful'.

John Walker

Don't Take Yourself Too Seriously

If I had my life to live over again, I'd try to make more mistakes next time.
I would relax, I would limber up, I would be sillier than I have been on this trip.
I know of very few things I would take seriously.
I would take more trips. I would be crazier.
I would climb more mountains, swim more rivers and watch more sunsets.
I would do more walking and looking.
I would eat more ice cream and less beans.
I would have more actual troubles and fewer imaginary ones.
You see, I'm one of those people who lives life prophylactically (protecting against disease) and sensibly hour after hour, day after day.
Oh, I've had my moments, and if I had to do it over again I'd have more of them.

In fact, I'd try to have nothing else, just moments, one after another, instead of living so many years ahead each day.

I've been one of those people who never go anywhere without a thermometer, a hot-water bottle, a gargle, a raincoat, aspirin, and a parachute

If I had to do it over again I would go places, do things, and travel lighter than I have.

If I had my life to live over I would start barefooted earlier in the spring and stay that way later in the fall.

I would play hooky more.

I wouldn't make such good grades except by accident.

I would ride on more merry-go-rounds

I'd pick more daisies.

A letter written by an anonymous friar
in a monastery in Nebraska

Films that inspired my faith
Of Gods and Men
Whistleblower
Into the Wild
5 Days of War
The Road

When we have nothing, and all is stripped away we find a holiness that delves deeper than we can know. Yet we still go back and fill the void with excess fashionable technology.

Vigilantes are the subjects of some extraordinary films (*The Dark Knight, Man on Fire, Harry Brown*) but where would Jesus be in such dark times?

Jesse Rowe

> 'You have to keep carrying the fire.'
> 'What fire?'
> 'The fire inside you.'
> From *The Road* by Cormack McCarthy

'Some people feel like they don't deserve love. They walk away quietly into empty spaces, trying to close the gaps of the past.'
Christopher McCandless

'God's place is all around us, it is in everything and in anything we can experience. People just need to change the way they look at things.'
Christopher McCandless

Jesse Rowe

'The sea's only gifts are harsh blows,
and occasionally the chance to feel strong. Now I don't know much about the sea, but I do know that that's the way it is here. And I also know how important it is in life not necessarily to be strong but to feel strong. To measure yourself at least once. To find yourself at least once in the most ancient of human conditions. Facing the blind death stone alone, with nothing to help you but your hands and your own head.'
Christopher McCandless

Jesse Rowe

> **'Never give up, never, never give up.'**
> Winston Churchill

'Every day you may make progress. Every step may be fruitful. Yet there will stretch out before you an ever-lengthening, ever-ascending, ever-improving path. You know you will never get to the end of the journey. But this, so far from discouraging, only adds to the joy and glory of the climb.'
Winston Churchill

Jesse Rowe

'Many of life's failures are people who did not realize how close they were to success when they gave up.'
Thomas Edison

> 'When facing a giant, don't say "He is so big, there is nothing I can do." Say "He is so big, I can't see how I can miss!"'
> J. John

Mountains of the mind are around us all everywhere. And it is when we test ourselves that we begin to know ourselves.

Faith sometimes feels like gym: through a combination of struggle, exhaustion and rest — we get weak in order to be made strong.

Jesse Rowe

> You cannot cross a sea by merely staring into the water.

Success seems to be largely a matter of hanging on in after others have let go.

> When life's problems seem overwhelming, look around and see what other people are coping with. You may consider yourself fortunate.

To guarantee success, act as if it were impossible to fail.

Jesse Rowe

You cannot change the seasons, or the wind, but you can change yourself.

> Enthusiasm is the greatest asset in the world. It beats money and power and influence. It is no more or less than faith in action.

All life is a chance. So take it! The person who goes furthest is the one who is willing to do and dare.

Jesse Rowe

Strength doesn't come from winning. Your struggles develop your strength

> You cannot be brave unless first you are afraid.

There is no feeling like coming home after danger.

> The greatest mistake you can make in life is to be continually fearing you will make one.

Jesse Rowe

Life's a game of ups and downs
and you're not always going to win. The real deal is how you handle the tough times when they come. And they will. Basically, there will come a point in time when something doesn't work out. That may even happen for a long period of time. Martin Luther King once said this; 'The measure of a man is not when he stands in moments of comfort and convenience, but when he stands at times of challenge and controversy.'

Carl Beech – cvm.org.uk

I can tell you, that there are loads of times when I've hit the wall and I've had my fair share of flack over the years. That's to be expected if you want to make your life count. In the words of my own Dad, 'Nothing ever happened to a bloke that didn't have a go.' He should know after a 30 year career in the police serving for the whole of his career as a detective and often armed in various elite squads. I learned from him that sometimes you just need to dust yourself off, spit out the grit and crack on!

Carl Beech – cvm.org.uk

As a man who follows Jesus,
I've however learned that my ability to crack on rests not in my own strength but in my identity as Gods son. Romans 8 v 15 says it all for me. I can remember a time when basically everything I had invested my life into was falling part around me. It was in that moment that I heard a small voice whisper to me. 'But it doesn't matter what people think or that your ideas and plans aren't working. What matters is that you are my son and I love you.' That was a massive game changer for me I can tell you. So just remember this when the tough times come. Keep looking up, crack on and remember that when all is said and done, win, lose or draw, with God as your strength and source of security you can have a go at changing the world.

Carl Beech – cvm.org.uk

I really don't trust people who are 'certain'.
I don't understand how anyone can live on this planet, which is bedevilled with pain and heartbreak, and have not the slightest doubt about professing faith in a God of love. As far as I'm concerned, faith isn't being 'certain': faith is being filled with doubt and deciding to believe anyway.

> Experience is something you don't get until just after you needed it.

God isn't 'nice' and neither is Jesus, and just the idea of the Holy Spirit is properly scary. The power of the authority of the kingdom of God and I get to submit petitions? If that doesn't make a man uncomfortable, he's an idiot.

Jim Chew

Either God is God or He isn't. Either He's in charge or He isn't. Start off with what you believe about God, and most other arguments will resolve themselves.

> Before you join in with an argument, ask yourself whether it actually matters or not.

God doesn't have to explain himself. He's God, and that means He doesn't have to answer questions.

Jim Chew

Jesus told us not to judge – and that includes ourselves. I have to give myself grace all the time and every day, mainly because I keep screwing things up.

> You are probably the most irritating person you know.

People keep saying to me that something is 'Biblical' - you can usually hear the capital 'B'. Aside from the fact that what they say is often nothing of the sort, is being 'biblical' a good thing? Rape and Genocide are biblical.

Jim Chew

There is always someone better than you, and always someone worse than you. (Be grateful for what you are. Learn to enjoy the success of others, and to encourage those not as able as you.)

> If the picture looks better than your wallpaper, then put it on the wall.

Do not wear yourself out to get rich.
Proverbs 23 v 4

Do not store up things for yourself without being rich towards God. Luke 12 v 21

Paul Hobbs

I love seeing the confidence of my four year old son with his own body. His jumping, running and dancing are so uninhibited and so inspiring to watch. I have regained confidence in my own body but I certainly didn't have that as a teenager, despite the strength and vitality of those years. I know that much of the confidence I did have came from my father's encouragement. It feels wonderful to affirm my own children as they grow - I pray that will help them through those years when our bodies change so quickly it's hard to feel we quite belong in them. What an awesome gift our bodies are.

Justin Tomkins

'Most men lead lives of quiet desperation.'
Henry David Thoreau

'The man who makes no mistakes does not usually make anything.'
Bishop W.C Magee

'How many people eat, drink and get married; buy, sell and build; make contracts and attend to their fortune; have friends and enemies, pleasures and pains, are born, grow up, live and die... but asleep!'
Joseph Joubert

'Seize the day, boys, seize the day. Make your lives extraordinary.'
From the movie *Dead Poets Society*

'You've got what it takes.'

'You cut the mustard.'

'You da'man!'

'I'm well chuffed with you.'

'You make the grade.'

'You are more than good enough.'

'Well done, mate.'

'I'm proud of you.'

'This is my boy and I'm so pleased with him.'

'Don't give up – you can do this.'

'You're great. The best.'

    What every boy and man wants to hear

Made in the USA
Charleston, SC
14 May 2014